## DATE DUE

# CATS ARE COOL

# AMERICAN SHORTHAIRS

by Gini Holland

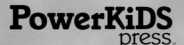
**PowerKiDS** press.

New York

Published in 2014 by The Rosen Publishing Group, Inc.
29 East 21st Street, New York, NY 10010

Produced for Rosen by Ruby Tuesday Books Ltd
Editor for Ruby Tuesday Books Ltd: Mark J. Sachner
US Editor: Sara Howell
Designer: Emma Randall

Photo Credits:
Cover, 1, 5, 6–7, 8–9, 11, 12–13, 14–15, 17, 22, 24–25, 30 © Shutterstock; 18–19, 20–21, 23 ©
Superstock; 27, 29 © Alamy; 28 © Rex Features.

Publisher Cataloging Data

Holland, Gini.
American shorthairs / by Gini Holland.
  p. cm. — (Cats are cool)
Includes index.
ISBN 978-1-4777-1277-1 (library binding) — ISBN 978-1-4777-1342-6 (pbk.) —
 ISBN 978-1-4777-1349-5 (6-pack)
1. American shorthair cat — Juvenile literature. I. Holland, Gini. II. Title.
SF449.A45 H65 2014
636.822—dc23

Manufactured in the United States of America

CPSIA Compliance Information: Batch #S13PK7 For Further Information contact: Rosen Publishing, New York, New York at 1-800-237-9932

# Contents

# A Class of Their Own

Many cats have short hair, but American shorthairs are a **breed** of cats that are in a class of their own. They are **purebred.**

This breed of cats comes in over 80 colors and patterns! Unlike mixed-breed cats, however, purebred American shorthairs always have kittens with the look, personality, and short hair length of the American shorthair breed.

American shorthairs are usually friendly with strangers and act loving with their owners. They have medium-long tails and are strong, healthy, and easy to care for.

In this book we will meet some beautiful American shorthairs and find out more about them. As you will see, they are pretty cool cats!

## Perfect Purr Facts

A purebred American shorthair is not cheap to buy. If you want to buy one of these cats, a kitten will usually cost between $500 and $1,000.

4

A young
American
shorthair cat

5

# The Mighty Mousers

American shorthairs are very good at catching mice. Their **ancestors**, shorthaired cats from Britain, were so good at hunting that North America's early English settlers brought them along on their ships.

The settlers needed good "mouser" cats to protect their food on the long trip across the ocean. When the settlers landed in North America, the British cats hopped off the boats, too.

These working cats kept mice out of homes and barns. Those strong enough to live through North America's hard winters had kittens. Many of these kittens grew up, found **mates**, and had kittens of their own. Over the years, each new **generation** of kittens was stronger and bigger than their British shorthair ancestors.

This cat is watching for mice in a barn.

The very first British ancestors of American shorthairs may have come over with the Pilgrims on the *Mayflower* in 1620. That's almost 400 years ago!

This ship is a replica, or copy, of the *Mayflower*.

# Old and New Names

Over time, these first American cats became a new breed of cat. At that time, they were called **domestic** shorthairs.

Some **cat fanciers** wanted to keep domestic shorthair cats purebred. They didn't want these American cats to get all mixed up with other kinds of cats. In the early 1900s, however, many people brought cats from other countries to the United States. These cats **mated** with domestic shorthairs. So cat fanciers carefully chose some cats that showed the look and personality of the first domestic shorthairs. They began to breed these together. In 1966, this breed was renamed the American shorthair.

**A purebred American shorthair**

A mixed
breed
domestic
shorthair

## Perfect Purr Facts

Today, shorthaired cats that aren't purebred but might be a mixture of different breeds are known as domestic shorthairs.

# Goldilocks Cats, Just Right!

**They're not too long, not too short, not too loud, and not too quiet. American shorthairs are just right!**

American shorthairs have strong bodies. A male may weigh up to 15 pounds when he is fully grown. An adult female will weigh about 8 to 12 pounds. American shorthairs have round faces with large eyes that give them a sweet look. They have square-shaped **muzzles** and strong jaws.

These cats are gentle and friendly, so they get along well with children, dogs, and other cats. They are great hunters, though, so keep them away from pet fish, gerbils, and rabbits.

American shorthairs usually live between 15 and 20 years.

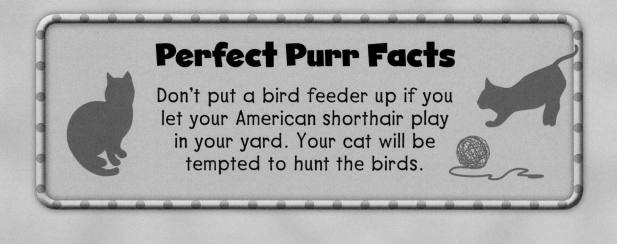

## Perfect Purr Facts

Don't put a bird feeder up if you let your American shorthair play in your yard. Your cat will be tempted to hunt the birds.

# Colorful Cats, Terrific Tabbies

American shorthairs come in white, black, cream, brown, silver, blue, which is a gray color, and gingery red. They also come in mixed color patterns.

Their best-known color pattern is called silver tabby. Silver tabbies have thick black markings on a silver background. Brown tabbies have black markings on a chocolate-brown background. Tabby patterns can look like bars or stripes around a cat's legs and body. Some tabbies have lines that make circles or spirals on their sides. Many have dark dots on their bellies.

The African wildcat is probably the oldest relative of both American shorthair and domestic shorthair cats. It gives us the tabby pattern we see in so many kinds of cats today.

**An African wildcat**

"M" on forehead

Stripes on legs

Silver tabby American shorthair kittens

## Perfect Purr Facts

Many tabbies have an "M" in the middle of their foreheads.

# Smokes, Calicoes, and Tortoiseshells

American shorthairs also come in patterns known as smoke, tortoiseshell, and calico.

No, a smoke has not been near a fire! It's just an American shorthair with a white undercoat. The tips of its fur are black, so it looks smoky.

**A tortoiseshell pattern**

Smokes are not as common as cats of other colors, so some cat fanciers like them best and think they are quite special. Many smokes have a tabby or other pattern, but their patterns don't show up much under their smoky color.

**A calico pattern**

A tortoiseshell American shorthair has patches of color rather than stripes. A calico has a three-colored pattern.

A smoke
American
shorthair
kitten

## Perfect Purr Facts

Sometimes the tabby and tortoiseshell patterns are found mixed together. Cats with this pattern are called torbies.

15

# True Mates

A female American shorthair may be ready to be a mother when she is six to ten months old. She will tell you by crying loudly. She wants to find a mate!

To breed a true American shorthair, you must let her mate with a male American shorthair. If she gets pregnant, her tummy will begin to look fatter.

In the last weeks of pregnancy, she will start to look for a quiet, dark place to nest. You will want to keep her inside so she doesn't nest outdoors. You can put a towel or blanket in a box and place it where she seems to want to nest.

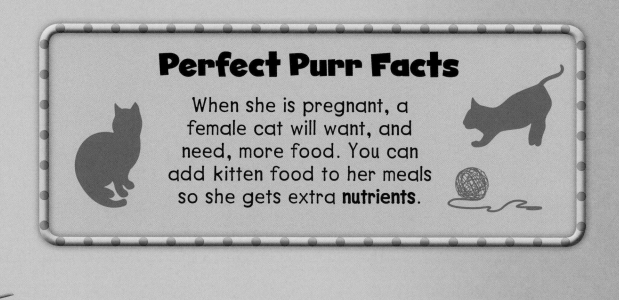

### Perfect Purr Facts

When she is pregnant, a female cat will want, and need, more food. You can add kitten food to her meals so she gets extra **nutrients**.

# Little Shorthairs

**As they grow up, American shorthair kittens will look a lot like their parents. When they are born, though, their eyes are not open and their fur is not fluffy.**

The kittens can't see, but they can smell! They sniff to find where to get milk from their mother. When they are a few days old, you can hear them purr as they drink. They open their eyes between five and eight days after birth. At about four weeks old, they are strong enough to walk, but they are still wobbly! They push and tumble over each other to feed. They snuggle together to keep warm.

New kittens' mothers will lick them clean. The kittens won't need to use a **litter box** until they start eating kitten food along with their milk, at about five weeks.

A four-week-old kitten

## Perfect Purr Facts

At about 12 weeks, a kitten is usually ready to go to a new home.

A mother American shorthair cat

A kitten drinking milk

19

# Taking Care of Your Cat

It's easy to take care of an American shorthair. Like all cats, they lick themselves clean all over, every day. Unlike longhairs, they don't need much brushing, but they do enjoy being brushed once in a while.

Brushing makes shorthairs' coats extra clean and pretty. You should brush your cat once or twice a week. American shorthairs may need a bath once or twice a year with cat shampoo in warm water.

They need clean drinking water and a high-quality cat food. You can ask your vet what kind is best. Be sure to get your cat's **vaccinations** and, unless you want to breed it, get it **altered** before it's old enough to mate.

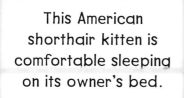
This American shorthair kitten is comfortable sleeping on its owner's bed.

## Perfect Purr Facts

You can give your American shorthair a basket or cat bed to sleep in, but don't be surprised if it curls up with you in bed at night. It likes the company and warmth!

# Outdoor Cat or Indoor Cat?

You be the judge. Most vets will tell you that cats should be kept indoors. Many owners agree. They say that indoor cats are safer than cats that are allowed outside.

Outdoor cats can catch more than mice! They can catch fleas, diseases, and infections if they get cuts. They can also get hit by cars. For these reasons, indoor cats may live longer than outdoor cats.

Other owners say that American shorthairs love the outdoors! They love to explore, hunt, and sleep in sunny or shady places. Their thick fur and hunting skills help protect them outdoors. Also, they can be vaccinated against diseases they could get from other animals.

There's always something to investigate indoors!

# Perfect Purr Facts

Some owners protect their cats outside with a safe mesh enclosure. It looks like a room-sized cage. Here, cats get to exercise and enjoy fresh air. After a few hours, the owners bring their cats indoors.

It's fun to explore outdoors!

# Best Cat of the Year

**Each year, the Cat Fanciers' Association (CFA) picks one Cat of the Year. For over 40 years, these have almost always been longhaired cats.**

Only eight shorthaired cats have won this title. Three have been American shorthairs! They had to be more than beautiful. They had to have great personalities, too. The first, in 1965, was named Shawnee Trademark. Then, in 1984, Hedgewood's Greatest American Hero won. Both Shawnee and Hero were silver tabbies.

In 1996, Sol-Mer Sharif became the first brown tabby to be named Cat of the Year. He was super friendly and seemed to love being in shows. In fact, he had won CFA's Best Kitten award in 1995, the year before, so his owners already knew he was great!

## Perfect Purr Facts

The Cat Fanciers' Association is an organization that arranges cat shows. Every year about 1,000 cats and kittens take part in its biggest show, the CFA International Cat Show. The competitors come to the United States from all over the world!

# Morris, the Picky Star

**Probably the most famous shorthair is Morris the Cat. This big orange tabby has starred in cat food commercials since the 1970s.**

In fact, Morris is not just one cool cat. Three different cats have played Morris! Are these cats true American shorthairs? Or are they domestic shorthairs with some American shorthair in them? Their picky eating habits make people think they must be purebred American shorthairs. Each Morris, however, was found at a shelter. No one knows who Morris's ancestors were.

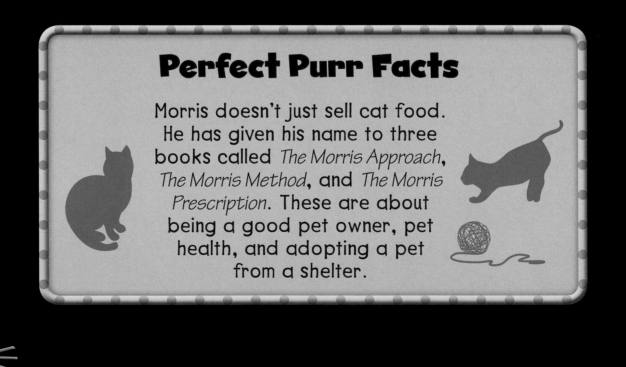

## Perfect Purr Facts

Morris doesn't just sell cat food. He has given his name to three books called *The Morris Approach*, *The Morris Method*, and *The Morris Prescription*. These are about being a good pet owner, pet health, and adopting a pet from a shelter.

# MORRIS
## The 9Lives® Cat

# Hardworking Cool Cats

**Many American shorthairs work in the movies. Two such cats played Azrael in *The Smurfs*, and the orange tabby, Milo, in *The Adventures of Milo and Otis*.**

As with Morris, it's hard to know for sure if these are purebred American shorthairs or domestic shorthairs with American shorthair in them. Whatever their history, these acting cats can climb and jump, and they have many adventures. Animal experts keep watch over the movie star cats to make sure they are treated carefully and don't get hurt.

In homes, the American shorthair is both a quiet, friendly pet and a "working cat." It will earn its keep in the house if mice try to move in. Inside the home or on the movie set, the American shorthair is one cool cat!

**Milo and Otis**

## Perfect Purr Facts

In *The Smurfs* actor Hank Azaria plays an evil wizard named Gargamel. Azrael is Gargamel's ginger cat. Hank Azaria said his cat costar was "a good kisser," but Hank admitted that he had to put cat food on his face to get his kiss!

Azrael

# Glossary

**altered** (OL-terd) An animal that has had an operation so it cannot have babies.

**ancestor** (AN-ses-ter) A relative that lived long ago.

**breed** (BREED) A type of cat or other animal. Also, the word used to describe the act of mating two animals in order to produce young.

**cat fanciers** (KAT FAN-see-erz) People who like, own, and sometimes breed cats.

**domestic** (duh-MES-tik) Tame and bred to live with humans.

**generation** (jeh-nuh-RAY-shun) The different ages, or layers, of a family. You are one generation, your parents are an earlier generation, and your grandparents are the generation that came before that.

**litter box** (LIH-ter BOKS) A shallow plastic box or tray filled with stony or sandy material that a cat uses as a bathroom.

**mate** (MAYT)  An animal's partner with which it produces young.

**mated** (MAYT-id)  Came together to produce young.

**muzzle** (MUH-zel)  The nose and mouth area of a cat, dog, and many other mammals.

**nutrients** (NOO-tree-ents) Substances that a living thing needs to help it live and grow. Foods contain nutrients such as vitamins.

**purebred** (PYUHR-bred)  An animal whose parents and ancestors were all bred from members of one breed.

**vaccinations** (vak-suh-NAY-shuhnz) Medicines that are usually given as shots that protect animals and people against diseases.

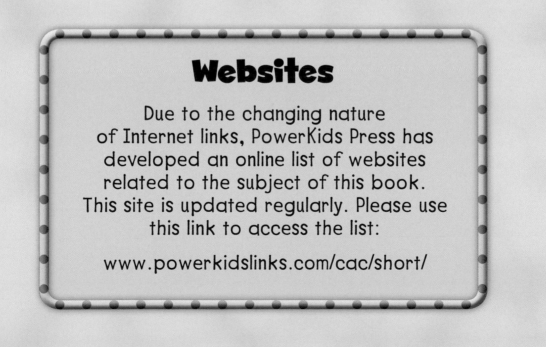

# Websites

Due to the changing nature of Internet links, PowerKids Press has developed an online list of websites related to the subject of this book. This site is updated regularly. Please use this link to access the list:

www.powerkidslinks.com/cac/short/

# Read More

**Landau, Elaine**. *American Shorthairs Are the Best!*. Best Cats Ever. Minneapolis, MN: Lerner Publishing Group, 2011.

**Perkins, Wendy**. *American Shorthair Cats*. Mankato, MN: Capstone Press, 2008.

**Rudolph, Jessica**. *American Shorthairs: Pioneers*. Cat-ographies. New York: Bearport Publishing, 2011.

# Index